Managing Your CIO Career

Steps That CIOs Have To Take In Order To Have A Long And Successful Career

"Practical, proven techniques that will help you to make your CIO career long and successful"

Dr. Jim Anderson

Published by:
Blue Elephant Consulting
Tampa, Florida

Copyright © 2013 by Dr. Jim Anderson

All rights reserved. No part of this book may be reproduced of transmitted in any form or by any means, electronic or mechanical, including photocopying, recording or by any information storage and retrieval system without written permission of the publisher, except for inclusion of brief quotations in a review.

Printed in the United States of America

Library of Congress Control Number: 2013920142

ISBN-13: 978-1493654307

ISBN-10: 1493654306

Warning – Disclaimer

The purpose of this book is to educate and entertain. This book does not promise or guarantee that anyone following the ideas, tips, suggestions, techniques or strategies will be successful. The author, publisher and distributor(s) shall have neither liability nor responsibility to anyone with respect to any loss or damage caused, or alleged to be caused, directly or indirectly by the information contained in this book.

Other Books By The Author

Product Management

- How To Have A Successful Product Manager Career: The Things That You Need To Be Doing TODAY In Order To Have A Successful Product Manager Career

- Product Manager Product Success: How to keep your product on track and make it become a success

Public Speaking

- Secrets To Planning The Perfect Speech

- Secrets To Organizing The Perfect Speech: How to organize the best speech of your life!

IT Manager Skills

- IT Manager Budgeting Skills

CIO Skills

- CIO Business Skills: How CIOs can work effectively with the rest of the company!

Negotiating

- Preparing For Your Next Negotiation: What You Need To Do BEFORE A Negotiation Starts In Order To Get The Best Possible Deal

Miscellaneous

- Power Distribution Unit (PDU) Secrets: What Everyone Who Works In A Data Center Needs To Know!

- Making The Jump: How To Land Your Dream Job When You Get Out Of College!

Acknowledgements

Any book like this one is the result of years of real-world work experience. In my over 25 years of working for 7 different firms, I have met countless fantastic people and I've been mentored by some truly exceptional ones. Although I've probably forgotten some of the people who made me the person that I am today, here is my attempt to finally give them the recognition that they so truly deserve:

- Thomas P. Anderson
- Art Puett
- Bobbi Marshall
- Bob Boggs

Dr. Jim Anderson

This book is dedicated to my wife Lori. None of this would have been possible without her love and support.

Thanks for the best 21 years of my life (so far)...!

Table Of Contents

CIOS DON'T HAVE TIME TO MANAGE THEIR CAREERS! 8

ABOUT THE AUTHOR 10

CONGRATULATIONS ON THE PROMOTION — YOU'RE IN TROUBLE NOW 14

ETHICS IS SOOO BORING – UNTIL YOU ARE GOING TO JAIL 17

SO YOU WANNA BE A CIO? HERE'S WHAT THEY LOOK LIKE... 21

5 SKILLS OF THE CIO OF THE FUTURE 25

HOW CAN A CIO (OR ANYONE ELSE) FIND A MENTOR? 29

WHAT IS THE #1 IT SKILL THAT A CIO NEEDS TO HAVE? 32

WHERE IS YOUR NEXT CIO COMING FROM? 35

WOMEN IN IT: WHAT'S THE CURRENT SCORE? 38

NEW NAME FOR CIOS: STRATEGIC EXECUTION OFFICER 41

A MENTOR NETWORK IS WHAT YOU NEED TO BECOME A CIO 45

HAS THE GLORY GONE OUT OF WORKING IN IT? 50

YOU DON'T DO A GOOD JOB AT MULTITASKING CIO, GET OVER IT .. 54

CIOs Don't Have Time To Manage Their Careers!

In today's fast-paced Information Technology (IT) field, Chief Information Officers (CIOs) are being asked to do more than ever. No longer is it enough to just make sure that the company's various servers and email systems are up and operating correctly, now CIOs have to play a role in setting the company's overall strategic direction.

It's all too easy for a CIO to get caught up in the day-to-day activities being of a modern IT executive and forget to do the most important job of all – manage their career. Recent studies have shown that the average tenure of a CIO is only four years!

If you want your career at your current company to be longer than that, then you need to start to take an active role in managing your career. It's not all about the technology (although that is important), rather managing your career is about managing relationships.

In order for a CIO to be successful, he or she needs to find the time to build the relationships both inside and outside of the company that are going to be needed in order allow their career to continue to progress.

One very important point that is all too easy to overlook is the fact that the skills that may have landed you the CIO job are not the skills that will be need to keep you in this job. What you're going to have to do is to develop an entirely new set of skills that allow the rest of the company to see just how valuable you are to the success of the firm.

The purpose of this book is to provide you with real-world examples of what a CIO has to do in order to successfully manage his or her career. There is no one answer to this question. Rather it requires a different way of thinking. You actually need to take the time to fully understand what the other people in the company want you to accomplish and then you're going to need to find ways show everyone just how valuable you are.

It is my hope that after having read this book you will be aware of the additional job that you've taken on as CIO – managing your career. Do this correctly and your CIO career will last a long time...!

Good luck!

- Dr. Jim Anderson, November, 2013

About The Author

I must confess that I never set out to be a CIO. When I went to school, I studied Computer Science and thought that I'd get a nice job programming and that would be that. Well, at least part of that plan worked out!

My first job was working for Boeing on their F/A-18 fighter jet program. I spent my days programming fighter jet software in assembly language and I loved it. The U.S. government decided to save some money and went looking for other countries to sell this plane to. This put me into an unfamiliar role: I started to meet with foreign military officials and I ended up having to manage groups of engineers who were working on international projects.

Time moved on and so did I. I found myself working for Siemens, the big German telecommunications company. They were making phone switches and selling them to the seven U.S. phone companies. The problem was that the switches were too complicated. Customers couldn't tell the difference between one complicated phone switch from another complicated phone switch. Once again I found myself working with the sales and marketing teams to find ways to make the great technology that the engineers had developed understandable to both internal and external customers.

I've spent over 25 years working as an senior IT professional for both big companies and startups. This has given me an opportunity to learn what it takes to manage and IT department in ways that allow it to maximize its output while becoming a valuable part of the overall company.

I now live in Tampa Florida where I spend my time managing my consulting business, Blue Elephant Consulting, teaching college courses at the University of South Florida, and traveling to work with companies like yours to share the knowledge that I have about how to create and manage successful IT departments.

I'm always available to answer questions and I can be reached at:

Dr. Jim Anderson
Blue Elephant Consulting
Email: jim@BlueElephantConsulting.com
Facebook: http://goo.gl/1TVoK
Web: http://www.BlueElephantConsulting.com/

"Unforgettable communication skills that will set your ideas free..."

Create IT Departments That Are Productive And A Valuable Asset To The Rest Of The Company !

Dr. Jim Anderson is available to provide training and coaching on the topics that are the most important to people who have to manage IT departments: how can I build a productive IT department (and keep it together) while at the same time providing the rest of the company with the IT services that they need?

Dr. Anderson believes that in order to both learn and remember what he says, speakers need to laugh. Each one of his speeches is full of fun and humor so that what he says "sticks" with everyone.

Dr. Anderson's CIO SkillsTraining Includes:

1. How to identify and attract the right type of IT workers to your IT department.
2. How to build relationships with the company's senior management in order to get the support that you need?
3. How to stay on top of changing technology and security issues so that you never get surprised?

Dr. Jim Anderson works with over 100 customers per year. To invite Dr. Anderson to work with you, contact him at:

Phone: 813-418-6970 or
Email: jim@BlueElephantConsulting.com

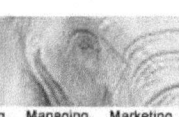
Speaking. Negotiating. Managing. Marketing.

Chapter 1

Congratulations On The Promotion — You're In Trouble Now

Congratulations On The Promotion — You're In Trouble Now

What if you just got promoted or accepted a new job. Plop — there you are. I've got some bad news for you, according to an article in the Harvard Business Review, in 2006 about 40% of the CIOs who left their jobs had lasted average of just 1.8 years.

If they can't hang on to their new jobs for very long, what makes you think that you can? It sure looks like you are going to have to quickly figure out what is going on so that you can start to show some value. Great — just how does one go about doing that?

First, just what is a new CIO supposed to figure out? Guess what — it's the same thing that a new CEO would need to determine: how to boost profitability, increase market share, overtake competitors, etc. Now the trick here is that a CEO and someone in IT will have different things that they control.

A CEO only really controls two things: hiring/firing and budgets. A CIO actually controls more: hiring/firing, technology selection, project progress, etc. The scope of their actions may differ; however, the goals are the same.

As a new CIO you will need to gather information quickly. You can expect to be given somewhere in the neighborhood of about 3-4 months to collect what you need. Be careful: most CIOs will start with whatever they know best. The problem is that the greatest improvements in your new area of responsibility may not come from the areas that you know best!

There are four guideposts that every new CIO needs to keep in mind when sizing up his new responsibilities:

1. Costs / prices will always decline

2. The company's competitive position determines your options

3. Customers and sources of profits don't stand still

4. Simplicity gets results

Using these four guideposts as you process the information that has been collected will allow you to identify the specific IT areas that are within your control for which changes will yield the greatest benefit for the firm.

At the end of the day, diagnosing the issue is only the first part of the process — next you need to decide where you want your team to go. In order to get there, you will need to define and implement initiatives based on your findings. Good luck!

Chapter 2

Ethics Is SOOO Boring – Until You Are Going To Jail

Ethics Is SOOO Boring – Until You Are Going To Jail

I don't know about you, but my eyes start to roll up into my head anytime I see an article with the word "ethics" in its title or if a speaker makes the mistake of saying *"... let's talk about ethics..."*. Yeah, yeah I know that this is the wrong attitude and that if I'm not careful I'll end up getting myself in trouble.

Or will I? I mean, I think that I'm smart enough to make the right decisions if push came to shove – aren't you? Kieran Mathieson over at Oakland University has spent some time thinking about this issue and he thinks that we are all in trouble.

There are really two parts to this discussion: how did we get here and why is ethics so hard for mere mortals to deal with? Dr. Mathieson points out in an article in the IEEE's Computer magazine that workers in the IT field basically see things in black & white: programs work or they don't.

We might argue about if Java is better than Ruby, but issues like this don't affect our core beliefs. However, ethics is a different issue. Ethics sneaks its way into everything that we do: choose a mate, raise children, do work, spend money, and vote. One of the big differences between the world of IT and the world of ethics is that ethics doesn't come with any rules – just what is the "correct" ethical decision in a given situation?

Would you have the guts to talk about ethics with your IT team? Yes, I know that the correct answer is a quick "Yes", but come on, would you really? I mean ethics questions have the ability to divide your team right down the middle. Oh, and if you've got a multicultural team, give it up – nobody will see a given ethical situation the same way.

So I swing back to my original point – ethics is quite boring until it's not. The reason that so many IT folks (Enron, Worldcom,

HealthSouth, etc.) find themselves on the wrong side of ethical decisions has a lot to do with how ethical situations show up.

Unfortunately they don't appear before us as someone handing us a gun and telling us to go shoot someone (with big flashing lights going off and sirens sounding). Nope, they sneak in around the edges of our lives.

How about this: your boss doesn't approve some meal that you had while traveling and so you end up paying for it. Feeling angry, you pad your next 5 expense reports in order to "get back what you are owed." But then things are just a bit tight at home, and so you keep padding your expense reports in more and more creative ways even after the original imagined offence has been repaid.

Later on, you are picking vendors for some small thing, let's say to supply paper for your printers. One of the vendors being considered takes you aside and says that if you select him, he'll provide you with a 10% discount off of his quoted price in cash once a month. He has a fairly good price and you might have selected him anyway. You are really only talking about a small amount of money, and you sure could use it right now with your bills starting to pile up. You look him in the eye and say "ok, but I would have selected you anyway" and somehow you feel better.

You feel even better when the cash starts showing up in an envelope mailed to your house each month. And so it goes… Can you see how a small ethical decision can open the door to much larger ethical violations? An avalanche starts very small, but in the end it can do a lot of damage.

So what's an IT person to do? Simple, practice, practice, practice. Every day we have opportunities to make countless ethical decisions (remember how it sneaks into all facets of our lives?). Recognizing that a decision is an ethical decision, no matter how small it seems to be, will help us to practice our decision making. Once we get onto the right ethical path for us, practice will help us to remain there.

Chapter 3

So You Wanna Be A CIO? Here's What They Look Like...

So You Wanna Be A CIO? Here's What They Look Like...

If your career plans call for you to one day to become a CIO (or if you already are), then it would be most helpful if you knew what a CIO looked like. I mean goodness gracious, if you walked into a room of IT professionals, wouldn't you want to be able to pick out the CIOs from the crowd?

If you know what a CIO looks like, then (if you're not one already) you will now have a clear action plan on what you need to do to transform yourself into one. If by chance you are already a CIO, then this is going to give you a great snapshot of what all of your peers look like.

If you measure up, then great – you should be sitting pretty. If you don't, then oh, oh – now you know where you have some work to do. The numbers that we're going to be talking about all come from the 2008 Ziff-Davis Enterprise CIO Role Survey so you know the data is probably fairly close to the truth.

Money, Money, Money: Let's start by talking about what everyone wants to know first – how much can I expect to be pulling in for all the grief that I'm going to have to put up with when I'm CIO? In base salary, you should be expecting to be taking home about $170,000. Not too bad, eh? Well it gets even better when you figure in your bonus that you'll be earning for completing that big ERP project on time and keeping the IT budget under control. You should be expecting a bonus of about $41,000. That means that you'll be pocketing right around $211,000 per year.

Details, Details, Details: Job satisfaction is all in the details, and this is no different for CIOs. First, let's ask the question – who's your boss? For 56% of CIOs the answer is the CEO (not bad; however, this means that 44% are NOT reporting to the big man...) What is your real job CIO? For 43% of you cost cutting is something that you consider to be your primary role. This is really bad news because there are a lot of other C-level executives that do this job much better than a CIO. Do you need an MBA to speak the language of business? Well, 31% of you thought that you did and so these folks went out and got themselves one of those MBA things. Finally, is this an all-boys club? Basically, yes. It turns out that only about 10% of CIOs are women. Ouch!

Purse Power: So it sounds rather girlish, but purse power is something that even the manliest of CIOs desperately wants more of. Each year a company launches many different projects. The CIO only has purse power control over a few of these projects so they are the most important to him/her. The two types of projects that a CIO is most likely to have control over are cross-functional process improvement projects (60% of CIOs have control over these) and technology adoption projects (90% of CIOs have control over these).

What Do You Do All Day?: The answer to this question turns out to really depend on what type of company you are CIO at. If you are a CIO at a big enterprise company, your top three roles are as follows:

1. Be an adviser on how to improve business processes.
2. Enable and execute business strategy
3. Coach other IT executives

Now if instead, you are working at a mid-market firm, then your top three roles will be different. Here's what they will look like for you:

1. Be an adviser on how to improve business processes.
2. Be a technology visionary – know what's coming and what it means to the firm.
3. Ensure that the company's existing technology works and keeps working correctly.

There you have it, a CIO's job defined in a nutshell. Now that doesn't seem so hard now does it?

Chapter 4

5 Skills Of The CIO Of The Future

5 Skills Of The CIO Of The Future

Psst – would you like a peek into the future? Sorry, I can't tell you when the financial markets are going to bottom out, when house prices will snap back, or even what lottery numbers would be a sure thing. However, I can tell you what the CIO of tomorrow is going to look like and he/she isn't going to look like the one that you've got right now!

As Rodeney Dangerfield said so elegantly, "*I can't get no respect*". This seems like it could almost be a mantra for CIOs. A survey of CIOs that Information Week is working on is starting to show some big problems up at the top of the IT career ladder. Specifically, outside of IT the other C-level executives aren't seeing the CIO as being all that useful and therefore the importance of the CIO has actually decreased over the past year. Oh, oh – this spells trouble for the rest of us.

So what's going on here? CIOs are falling down in several areas. Either they are going to have to find ways to fix their performance in these areas or they are going to have to step aside and let someone else take the wheel of the IT shop. Here's a list of what today's CIOs need to fix in order to start getting some respect:

1. **Spend Money The Right Way:** One of the biggest gripes that the rest of the company has about CIOs is that they are too caught up in performing support tasks. This means that too much of a CIOs budget is being spent on the wrong stuff: support, not innovation. Right now the split seems to be 70% being spent on support and 30% being spent on new initiatives. What does the rest of the company want? How about a 20% / 80% split? I don't want to hear that that's impossible – get cracking CIO!

2. **Know Your Technology:** It sure seems like there is no shortage of new technology constantly cropping up. The

rest of the company wants the CIO to be on top of all of this technology stuff, sort through it, and tell them what's important and what's not.

The CIO needs to be a technology visionary that the rest of the company can turn to in order to find out what's real and what's not. Case in point: the converged network (voice, video, and data on one network instead of three separate networks) was big a few years ago. Your CIO should have been all over that.

Right now Cloud Computing appears to be the next big thing in whatever form it ends up taking. Your CIO should be leading the charge to find out what this will eventually mean for your company.

3. **Talk The Talk (of Business):** This is one that's been hanging around for a while, but it just won't go away. CIOs need to stop talking tech with other C-levels and start to talk about solving business problems. It is the responsibility of the CIO to translate technology into business terms and use that to talk with other business executives.

4. **Execute, Execute, Execute:** Quick – think of two words that describe your IT department. Did you pick "expensive" and "slow"? If not, then perhaps you should have because that is how everyone else thinks of you.

The ability to deliver on promises made by the IT department is a key part of any CIOs job. The CIO of tomorrow needs to ensure that if the IT department says that it's going to do something, then it follows through and delivers what it promised on time.

5. **It's All About The Processes:** Ultimately the rest of the company is looking to the CIO in order to get help in further automating the way that the business operates. Nobody really cares if you're going to use Web 2.0 technologies, SaaS, SOA, etc. What matters is that what once was done manually and took a long time can now be done automatically and takes much less time.

Chapter 5

How Can A CIO (Or Anyone Else) Find A Mentor?

How Can A CIO (Or Anyone Else) Find A Mentor?

I'm sure that you've heard from many other places that you need a mentor. Mentoring is like that networking thing. You know that it's probably a good thing to be doing. However, you're not quite sure how to get started with it and so it seems to always end up on your "should do" list where, of course, it never gets done.

The world has become a complicated place and no matter how much you learned in school or on the job, there is no way that you could possibly know it all. CIOs and anyone who works in IT these days really needs a mentor – do you have one?

A traditional mentoring relationship was when an older colleague would talk a younger colleague under their wing and they would show you the ropes and maybe even open some doors for you along the way. Bad news: those days are pretty much over at this point in time.

Today mentors need their own mentors in order to keep up with all the changes that are occurring in technology, globalization, workplace diversity, etc. Since the old way of mentoring is now officially broken, you are going to need a new way of getting the guidance that mentoring used to provide.

A clever solution to this problem is instead of limiting yourself to one mentor, develop a small network of mentors – each having a particular area of specialty. Keep in mind that mentors for this "personal board of directors" do not need to come from where you work: professional societies, university, friends, all are potential candidates. Here are 5 steps that will help you build your mentor network:

1. **First Look In The Mirror:** How can you ask others to help you unless you know what kind of career help you need? Spending time listing out your strengths and

weaknesses is the best way to decide what kind of mentors you need.

2. **Determine What Your Needs Are:** Once you know what your strengths and weaknesses are, then you are ready to decide what steps you need to take in order to achieve your goal. If you are a CIO already, then you may want to become CEO as a next step. If you want to be CIO, then you probably need to first be a Director, next an Executive Director, and so on. Knowing this type of information will help you to understand what types of mentors can give you the coaching that you'll need in order to get promoted.

3. **Pick Your Mentors:** Instead of waiting around for a kindly Sr. Executive (at your company or perhaps at another company) to reach out and offer to coach you (just like in the movies), you need to select those whom you will invite to be your mentors. Remember that mentoring has to be a two-way street so make sure that you have something to give back to the people that you ask to mentor you.

4. **Weed & Sow Constantly:** As time goes by, your mentoring needs will change. This means that you need to be constantly re-evaluating who is currently in your mentoring network. Over time your needs will change and you will need to gracefully swap out board members.

5. **Give More Than You Receive:** Keep in mind that mentoring is a two-way street. Ultimately you will want to be sought out by others to be their mentor so that you can learn from the best and the brightest. The only way to make sure that this happens is to develop a reputation for being a great mentor yourself.

Chapter 6

What Is The #1 IT Skill That A CIO Needs To Have?

What Is The #1 IT Skill That A CIO Needs To Have?

Today's CIOs are expected to have many more sets of skills than those that they followed did. One can only suspect that the CIOs of tomorrow will be faced with even higher expectations. Cloud computing, outsourcing, insourcing, business alignment, top line growth, bottom line growth – which one is the most important to know the most about? It turns out that the answer is none of these.

A little secret that nobody ever talks about is that the higher in an organization that you rise, the less "real work" you actually get to do. Many first time CIOs struggle with this new reality – they are the ones who can't help but do the work of those that they manage.

Jack Welch probably said it best in his biography **Jack: Straight from the Gut** when he said that as CEO of GE, really all he was able to do was to hire and fire people and approve budgets – that's it! CIOs are in the same situation, so what is the #1 skill that they must have?

Simple, the ability to reach conclusions when all that they have to work with is ambiguous evidence. Think about it for a moment, all of the information that a CIO gets has been heavily filtered by the rest of the IT organization. If there are any unpopular opinions, then they have probably been censored before reaching the CIO. All slanted or partisan viewpoints have been masked as objective arguments. There is even the possibility that honest mistakes have been made.

CIO's need to have a type of analytical rigor that will allow them to make sense of the information that is presented to them. This is the skill that will allow them to sort through all of the information that crosses their desk and will allow them to dive down and finally get to the real story.

The big question for tomorrow's CIOs is how can you get the bottom of things when all that you have to work with is incomplete information? How can you present yourself to your colleagues and to your IT department as an authentic IT leader in such a way that others will be willing to follow you?

One of the most dangerous things that can mislead a CIO is his/her own opinion. Sure we all have an opinion; however, if we pre-judge a situation and reach our own opinion too quickly then we can find ourselves falling into a pattern of belief. We may do this because it's simple to do or because it fits some particular social need.

However, the problem with our opinions is that they don't necessarily have to be true. If a CIO chooses to believe something because of just the information that has been presented to him/her, then it's going to be very hard to get him/her to surrender that belief.

Too many of us like to say that we keep an open mind when we really don't. In order to be an effective CIO both today and tomorrow, we're going to need to make sure that we work very hard to make good decisions. This means that we've got to realize that we will never have complete information. What we need to do is find ways to use the partial information that we have to get to the bottom of the issues. Then, and only then, will we be effective CIOs.

Chapter 7

Where Is Your Next CIO Coming From?

Where Is Your Next CIO Coming From?

So here's the scenario: a previously unknown meteor comes streaking down to earth and somehow lands squarely on top of your CIO squashing him/her instantly. What do you do next? Where would your replacement CIO come from and do you know who that would be?

A study conducted by the equipment supply firm CDW has revealed that even at firms with 1,000 or more employees, 38% of them did not have a formal CIO succession plan. Ouch – watch out for those meteors!

Even if your CIO doesn't spend a lot of time outside where there might be meteors, a good point to keep in mind is that the average tenure of a CIO is 3-5 years. When you start to think about who might replace your current CIO, one question comes to mind immediately: internal vs. external.

It really doesn't help matters that exactly what the qualifications to be CIO are can be quite subjective. In most cases it really depends on several factors including the size of your company, what industry you play in, and what the current expectations of the IT department are.

A study done by Information Week revealed that of 500 current CIOs, 58% of them were recruited from the outside. This means that choosing the outsider is not all that unusual.

When it comes down to deciding if you should be looking internally vs. externally, company culture can play a big role. If your firm has a history of hiring from the outside, then getting your next CIO from there will feel much more natural.

Internal candidates can be a great way to go because they already know so much about the company. At the same time, they often find themselves in a situation in which they are in over their heads in responsibilities. External CIO candidates often have the experience to do the job; however, simply because they come from the outside expectations will be higher for them.

In the end make sure that you choose carefully from all of your potential sources – you're going to need the best possible talent in your top IT spot.

Chapter 8

Women In IT: What's The Current Score?

Women In IT: What's The Current Score?

How many women work in your IT department? Is your CIO a woman? The answer to the first question is probably "**not that many**", and the answer to the second is all too often "**no**". We've been aware that this is an issue for a while, how are we doing on addressing it?

How Do Women Feel About Working In IT?

One of the best places to start when we are trying to figure out where things currently stand is to ask the women who are currently working in IT how it's going. Rob Preston over at InformationWeek did some data collection and he discovered a study on this topic that was released by a women's professional organization called Catalyst.

The study revealed that women working in the IT field were **basically satisfied** with both their jobs and where they worked. However, there are still big issues when it comes to how they interact with their **bosses**, how **fair** they think decision making is, and how much of an opportunity they have to participate in **planning**.

How Many Female CIOs Do We Have?

We've got more today than we had 5 years ago; however, there are only about **75 female CIOs** in InformationWeek's top 500 companies (that comes out to be about 15%). This list includes:

- Kathy Owen – Unum
- Marina Levinson – NetApp
- Beth Perlman – Constellation Energy
- Leslie Jones – Motorola

There's been improvement, but there is still a long way to go.

What Tech Companies Do A Good Job Of Promoting Women?

This is where the rubber meets the road. Any company can talk a good line about how much they support diversity; however, promoting someone into the senior management ranks means that you think that they have the best chance of **driving revenue**. Here's how the familiar tech names stack up:

- HP – 21% of senior executives are women
- Oracle – 18%
- IBM – 13%
- Google – 13%
- Cisco – 11%
- Microsoft – 11%
- Dell – 0%

Oh my – did you see that Dell number? There is **no excuse** for that – women make up too much of the total IT workforce today for any company to be that unbalanced.

The Next Steps

So should IT departments start to institute mandatory gender based promotions so that 51% of their senior staff are female? No, that's not the correct solution. In the end, what we all want is **the best people** leading the company independent of gender.

IT may always be just a bit "male heavy" because of the nature of the beast. However, for any company to succeed, you need to make sure that **everyone** has a chance at the top spots and you need to make sure that you have a bench of capable employees that is made up of **all genders.** That's the secret to real long-term success.

Chapter 9

New Name For CIOs: Strategic Execution Officer

New Name For CIOs: Strategic Execution Officer

In order to complete in a global economy that is moving faster every day, more and more firms are committing to implementing those really BIG process digitization projects. More often than not the CIO will find himself / herself in charge of not only the implementation of the new software application, but also **the overall success of the project**. How do you go about doing that?

What Goes Wrong With Big IT Projects

We all know the statistics – most big IT projects are not successful. However, the key question is why? It turns out that all too often the issue is not with the new process automation technology that is being implemented, but rather with **the management challenge** that comes along with a project like this.

The reason that managing a large transformational IT project is so hard is because the CIO also needs to be finding ways to drive **the new business process changes** that will be required once the new systems have been installed. It turns out that nobody likes change!

What Doesn't Work?

It seems as though IT departments have been trying since the beginning of time to find a way to tackle this **two-headed IT project beast**. One approach has been to give responsibility for the success of the project to an **executive governance committee**. It turns out that this type of committee does an excellent job of defining the strategy for implementing the changes that will be needed, but does a lousy job of executing it.

Another approach has been to create an **IT task force** to implement this type of change. They generally do a good job of getting the new application up and running, but they lack the wide-ranging authority to cause other parts of the company to change how they are doing their jobs.

What Does An IT Strategic Execution Officer Do?

If the CIO is willing to step up and tackle leading both sides of a major IT process automation project, just what do they have to do? There are **three fundamental tasks** that they will need to deal with:

- Implementing the process automation application(s).

- Making sure that the new technology gets adopted by the rest of the company.

- Making sure that the new processes that the project has implemented start to get used by everyone.

Ultimately, the CIO will be filling the **management / leadership gap** that exists between coming up with the process automation plan and actually changing the company to use the project once it has been implemented.

Final Thoughts

No CIO wants to take on more work – there's not enough time in the day to get everything done as it is. However, ensuring that big IT projects get implemented correctly and that the company transforms its processes in order to use the new tool is the key to the company's **long term success**.

This is a clear example of where a CIO gets to practice for his / her next job: becoming CEO. Nobody else will be as well positioned to implement cross-company changes. CIOs who can pull this off will have **found a way** to apply IT to enable the rest of the company to grow quicker, move faster, and do more.

Chapter 10

A Mentor Network Is What You Need To Become A CIO

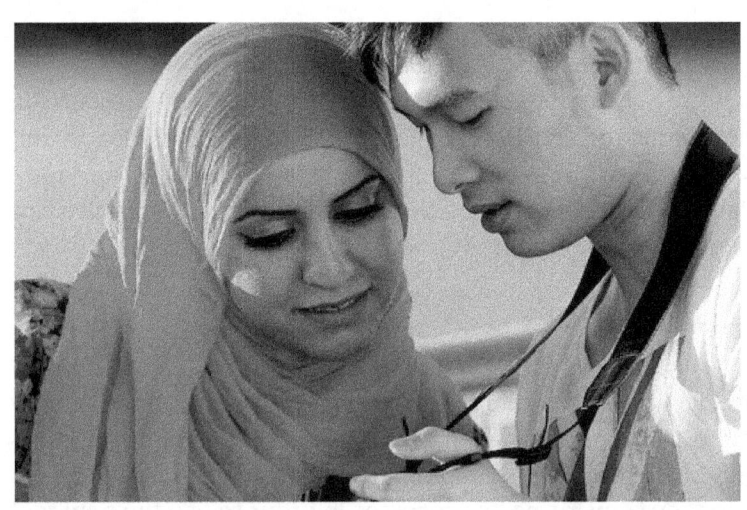

A Mentor Network Is What You Need To Become A CIO

I've got a quick question for you: what is the next step in your career? What do you want to **get promoted to**? In fact, as long as we are talking about that, what comes after THAT promotion? If you want to become a CIO, then career ladder generally goes: IT worker, manager, director, executive director, CIO, and then perhaps CEO. Got a plan on how you are going to get to that next step?

The Problem With Career Mentors

It used to be that what you needed in order to climb out of an IT position was a **mentor** - someone who would take you under their wing and guide you during your career. Bad news – those days are long gone.

It wasn't that there was anything wrong with the old way, it's just that the **world started to move faster**. Nowadays nobody stays in a given position long enough to act as a mentor to you for any reasonable length of time. Even if they did, they are probably too busy to spend enough time with you keeping your career on track.

The old way of picking a mentor and having them work with you over time to shape and guide your career is gone – things move too fast and change too often to allow this to work anymore. Instead, you need to discover how to create **networks of mentors** that they can use to provide the career guidance that you will need over the years.

If you thought the old way was **tough**, just wait until you try to figure out how to do things using the new way!

The New Way Of Managing Your Career

Dr. Dawn Chandler (CA Polytech State University), Dr. Douglas Hall (Boston University) and Dr. Kathy Kram (Boston University) have spent some time looking into **this problem** with the modern workplace and they've got some ideas about how we can fix things.

Since there is really no way for you to get a single individual to agree to act as your mentor for the 40-45 years that your IT career is going to last, instead you are going to have to take a different approach. You are going to have to **create a network of mentors** that you can use to accomplish what you need to get done.

Oh, there is one small problem with this clever solution: most of us are **not all that good** at creating a mentor network like this let alone trying to maintain it. It looks like you are going to need some suggestions on how best to do this.

Building And Maintaining A Mentor Network

One of the first things that you are going to have to realize about building your mentor network is that the people that you are going to ask to be a part of your network will not all be the same. This means that you are going to have develop a **special set of skills** in order to be able to (1) find them, and (2) create relationships with them that will make them want to mentor you.

Here is what you are going to have to do in order to **create a mentoring network** that will help your IT career move to the next level:

- **Talk, Talk,Talk** - you are going to have to be willing to take the initiative and reach out to those people that you want to be a part of your mentoring network – they aren't going to contact you. Once you've contacted them for the first time, then you are going to have to work at maintaining contact with them so that they don't forget about you.

- **Be Sensitive** – Not everyone that you talk to is going to want to be your mentor. It's going to be up to you to take the time to pick up on the message that they are sending your way. Few people will actually come out and say "no", so it's up to you to detect those folks who would like to decline the opportunity.

- **It's The Takeoff That Counts** – when you've found someone who is willing to be a member of your mentor network, then you've got to be willing to make an extra effort to make sure that your initial interactions with that person go very well. They will set tone for the rest of your relationship. Show up early for meetings, follow up quickly on actions, and pay attention when they are talking.

- **Be Prepared** – make sure that you get ready for every meeting with someone who is in your mentor network. Research what you want to ask them, make sure that you can show that you are making progress in your career, and come prepared to ask questions about challenges that you are currently facing.

- **Information Is The Key** – you need to be willing to share information with your mentoring network. This does not mean that you have to tell them all the details about what you had for breakfast today, but rather that you are willing to lay out your current challenges and failures that you've had – you know, stuff that can be hard to talk about.

- **It's A Two-Way Street** – if someone agrees to be a part of your mentoring network, then you have agreed to do your best to help them out also. This means that you have a responsibility to help your mentors out whenever you have an opportunity to do so. This can be as simple as passing on information that you run across to actually doing work for them.

- **Be A Nice Person** – Nobody want to work with a jerk and they certainly don't want to mentor one. No matter what kind of day you've had, always be on your best behavior when you interact with a member of your mentor network.

- **Be Positive** – how you choose to view the world is a key part of how others see you. If you have a positive attitude you will naturally attract people to your mentor network and you'll be able to keep them there. If you've got a negative attitude, then nobody is going to want to lend you a helping hand.

Final Thoughts

As a member of an IT department, you are undoubtedly busy. However, it turns out that you have yet **another job** on top of your "day job" – managing your career. You can't do this by yourself and so you're going to need to have someone guide you – a mentor network.

Creating and maintaining a mentor network is no easy task. However, if you go about doing it in the right way it can become a powerful force that will cause your career to shoot ahead and make sure that you don't get left behind.

CIOs (and those who want to become a CIO) who are able to build and maintain a good network of mentors will boost their careers and by doing so will have **found a way** to apply IT to enable the rest of the company to grow quicker, move faster, and do more.

Chapter 11

Has The Glory Gone Out Of Working In IT?

Has The Glory Gone Out Of Working In IT?

Why did you decide to go to work in the IT field? I can really only speak for myself, but there was a bit of glamour to the IT field when I entered it. Everything seemed to be so shiny and new and change was happening so fast that you just knew that this was going to be **"the place"** to be in order to have a great career. Is that still true or has something fundamental changed about our profession?

What Tom Siebel Thinks About IT Today

Randall Stross over at the New York Times ran across a speech that **Tom Siebel** (founded Siebel Systems, made Billions of $) gave to some Stanford engineering students about the current state of the IT industry.

Basically Tom said that he feels that IT has become a **mature industry**. He expects that going forward it will be growing at a rate that is no faster than the overall economy. What he was really saying is that he thinks that IT's glory days are behind it. In fact, he thinks that the party was over as of about 2000.

What Happened To IT?

Siebel has gone back and run the IT industry growth numbers. It is his belief that there were about 20 years from **1980 to 2000** in which the IT industry experienced runaway growth rates that averaged out to about 17%.

Why has it all stopped? Siebel believes that we've accomplished what we set out to do: "the promise of the post-industrial world has been realized."

Furthermore, Tom believes that what remains to be done really is not all that exciting(!)

Re-Looking At The Numbers

Stross reached out to Dr. Shane Greenstein at Northwestern University and asked him to relook at the IDC numbers. Good news for all of us working in IT, Dr. Greenstein has drawn some different conclusions about where IT stands than Siebel did.

It turns out that if you take a close look at IDC's annual IT spending estimates, they show that there was a 11.6% spending rate from 1980 – 2000 instead of 17%. I'm not sure if this information is going to make you happy, but it does point out that Siebel's numbers were just a bit off.

What was even more interesting about this second pass at crunching the IT growth numbers is that it turns out that the most golden years of IT were in the 1960's. The reason that this was the best period of grow was because it was when the use of mainframe computers spread widely. Way back in the years from 1961 to 1971 the compounded annual growth rate was 35.7%. That's why IBM got to be so big!

Final Thoughts

Look, IT is (still) a great field to be working in. Yeah, yeah if you look at certain reports it can look like the growth rate of the IT field is starting to go down. However, you need to remember something very important: declining growth rates over time are to be expected – it doesn't take many sales to show huge percentage gains when the base is small.

I don't know about you, but I'm going to take comfort in the fact that when the economy recovers, there is no dearth of **unfinished projects** for IT. Now that's going generate some serious growth in the IT field!

CIOs who believe that IT's glory days are still ahead of it and who don't get held back by reports of declining IT industry growth numbers will continue to look for ways to apply IT to enable the rest of the company to **grow quicker, move faster, and do more**.

Chapter 12

You Don't Do A Good Job At Multitasking CIO, Get Over It

You Don't Do A Good Job At Multitasking CIO, Get Over It

Too little time, too much to do. Does that adequately describe your CIO job? I don't know about you, but often is the time that I've looked with envy at my peers who are great **multitaskers** and wished that I could be more like them. It turns out that I was wishing for the wrong thing – multitaskers actually do a **lousy job** at just about everything.

The Study

Ruth Pennenaker reports that some researchers at Stanford University have just completed a groundbreaking study on **people who multitask**. You know who you are – you're talking on the phone even as you are answering emails and zipping off text messages on you iPhone all at the same time. Oh how I have so wanted to be you!

The researchers found that most persistent multitaskers actually **performed badly** in a variety of tasks that they were asked to do. As the researchers dove deeper to find out why the multitaskers were doing so badly, what they found was that they don't do a very good job of focusing on what they are trying to do. This also means that they are much more likely to get distracted while they are trying to perform a task. On top of all this, the study showed that they are actually weaker than non-multitaskers at shifting between tasks and organizing the information that they collect.

Results Of The Study

My favorite part of the study is where the researchers discovered that people who are always multitasking are actually **worse** at multitasking than those of us who ordinarily don't multitask!

When the study was started, the researchers started with the idea that multitaskers have some characteristic that makes them **better at multitasking** than regular folks. What they discovered is that multitaskers are just pretty much lousy at doing everything.

One of the researchers was quoted as saying "We kept looking for multitaskers' advantages in this study. But we kept finding only disadvantages. We thought multitaskers were very much in control of information. It turns out, they were just **getting it all confused**."

However, doesn't it LOOK like multitaskers are always busy? Shouldn't that mean that they must be getting more done than the rest of us who just can't do that much all at the same time? It turns out that high multitaskers are "**suckers for irrelevancy**". Simply put, sure they are doing things, but what they are working on more often than not really doesn't matter.

A Personal Multitasking (Failure) Story

I firmly fall into the "not a good multasker" camp and I should know it. However, every once in a while I try my hand at multitasking, generally with **disastrous results**. Allow me to share my most recent story:

I was **late for a doctor's appointment** and yet I had a conference call that I needed to participate in (not just listen to). I jumped into the car, programmed the Garmin GPS system with the doctor's office address, stuck my Blackberry headset in my ear, and set the Garmin on "mute" so that it wouldn't interfere with my conference call.

As I hurtled down the highway in the far left lane at about 70 mph jabbering away in an animated conversation on the conference call, I happened to look over at the Garmin and noticed that it was signaling that I needed to be **taking the exit** that I was just about to pass by (remember that I had been smart enough to mute it so I had no warning). Oh, oh.

A non-multitasking person would have realized that (1) I had already gone too far past the exit to make it, (2) I was in the wrong lane to try to make the exit, (3) I was going too fast to make the exit. In my multitasking state, I **realized none of this** and I attempted to go for it.

I didn't make it. I was going too fast and I was too far past the exit to have ever had any chance of making it. What I ended up doing was **plowing headfirst** into the aluminum guardrails which were anchored to solid 4"x4" chunks of wood. I probably hit them going a good 40 mph despite having tried to stand on the brakes once I realized what was going to happen.

Thanks to seatbelts and airbags, I walked away without a scratch. However, the car was a **total loss**. Oh, and I got a $100+ ticket from the police for basically being a bad driver. I say once again – I can't multitask!

Final Thoughts

CIOs who multitask will **perform at a lower level** than those who focus on one task at a time. Although this seems to fly in the face of everything that we've seen in our workplace (don't multitaskers get all of the promotions?), you can't argue with research results.

Should you try to convince your friends and peers who are multitaskers to stop doing it because it just doesn't work? No. The core of the problem is that not only do multitaskers **think they're great at what they do**; they've also convinced everybody else they're good at it too.

Ultimately those of us who are not multitaskers will be able to show better results for how we've spent our time. If we can make sure that the rules of the game that we're playing are **all about results** and not appearances, then the non-multitaskers will win every time.

CIOs who can focus on one task at a time and do it well instead of trying to do multiple tasks at the same time poorly will be better at finding ways to apply IT to enable the rest of the company to **grow quicker, move faster, and do more**.

Hard work does not
guarantee success;
However, success does
not happen
without hard work.

- Dr. Jim Anderson

Create IT Departments That Are Productive And A Valuable Asset To The Rest Of The Company !

Dr. Jim Anderson is available to provide training and coaching on the topics that are the most important to people who have to manage IT departments: how can I build a productive IT department (and keep it together) while at the same time providing the rest of the company with the IT services that they need?

Dr. Anderson believes that in order to both learn and remember what he says, speakers need to laugh. Each one of his speeches is full of fun and humor so that what he says "sticks" with everyone.

Dr. Anderson's CIO SkillsTraining Includes:

4. How to identify and attract the right type of IT workers to your IT department.
5. How to build relationships with the company's senior management in order to get the support that you need?
6. How to stay on top of changing technology and security issues so that you never get surprised?

Dr. Jim Anderson works with over 100 customers per year. To invite Dr. Anderson to work with you, contact him at:

Phone: 813-418-6970 or
Email: jim@BlueElephantConsulting.com

Speaking. Negotiating. Managing. Marketing.

Photo Credits:

Cover - By: Reno Tahoe

http://www.flickr.com/photos/renotahoe/

Chapter 1 - By: Calsidyrose

http://www.flickr.com/photos/calsidyrose/

Chapter 2 - By: ॐ Didi ॐ

http://www.flickr.com/photos/dey/

Chapter 3 - By: Rafael Anderson Gonzales Mendoza

http://www.flickr.com/photos/andercismo/

Chapter 4 - By: Max California

http://www.flickr.com/photos/42650760@N08/

Chapter 5 - By: chaines106

http://www.flickr.com/photos/26346563@N04/

Chapter 6 - By: churl han

http://www.flickr.com/photos/churl/

Chapter 7 - By: Gerard Stolk

http://www.flickr.com/photos/gerardstolk/

Chapter 8 - By: William Petruzzo

http://www.flickr.com/photos/petruzzophoto/

Chapter 9 - By: Coen Dijkman

http://www.flickr.com/photos/cone_dmn/

Chapter 10 - By: Play Among Friends Paf

http://www.flickr.com/photos/playamongfriends/

Chapter 11 - By: Mark

http://www.flickr.com/photos/bigblue/

Chapter 12 - By: Thomas Hawk

http://www.flickr.com/photos/thomashawk/

www.ingramcontent.com/pod-product-compliance
Lightning Source LLC
Chambersburg PA
CBHW071816170526
45167CB00003B/1328